WOLVERHAMPTON
PAST & PRESENT

Queen Square and Lichfield Street, 1960. The arrival of the Mander Centre put an end to the Queen's Arcade seen on the right and the Queen's Cinema has disappeared beneath an extension to the neighbouring bank. The road has been realigned several times and Prince Albert's statue has moved, but there is still something enduring about this view that expresses continuity as well as change. *(Bill Bawden)*

WOLVERHAMPTON
PAST & PRESENT

NED WILLIAMS

WHSmith

First published in the United Kingdom in 2002 by
Sutton Publishing Limited exclusively for
WHSmith, Greenbridge Road, Swindon SN3 3LD

British Library Cataloguing in Publication Data
A catalogue record for this book is available from the British Library.

ISBN 0-7509-3166-3

Illustrations

Front endpaper: The staff of the Cash Bakery on an outing in 1934. They have assembled outside the premises at 1 Penn Road and are awaiting their charabanc. *(Geoff Pocock)*
Back endpaper: A bunch of local 'Westerners' calling themselves Cowboys on Wheels raise money for charities. They 'starred' at the 2002 Wolverhampton City show in West Park.
Half title page: A portrait of Wulfrunian Samuel Turner and his dog Prince. They are sitting on the doorstep of 4 Wharf Street, Horseley Fields, in 1932. *(Sheila Edwards' collection)*
Title page: A Metro tram coming off the Whalebone Bridge into Wolverhampton in 2002, 100 years after Wolverhampton's first electric tram travelled down Cleveland Road. *(Ned Williams)*

Typeset in 11/14pt Photina and produced by
Sutton Publishing Limited, Phoenix Mill,
Thrupp, Stroud, Gloucestershire GL5 2BU.
Printed and bound in England by
J.H. Haynes & Co. Ltd, Sparkford.

Contents

The Mayor of the City of Wolverhampton, 2002–3, Councillor Robert Hart surrounded by paintings of his predecessors recently rediscovered in the Civic Centre. On the extreme left is Mayor J. Ford, on the floor on either side of Councillor Hart are Mayor Crowther Smith and his Mayoress (1865–6). Sharing the sofa with Councillor Hart is Mayor Isaac Jenks who donated the chain of office, bearing the old coat of arms. On the right is Mayor Wynn (1852–3) and on the extreme right is Mayor James Longman (1867–8). These pictures are currently being restored and reframed. *(Ned Williams)*

Foreword

By Councillor Robert Hart, Mayor of Wolverhampton

As mayor of our newly created city, I am delighted to write this foreword as an acknowledgement of the continuing greatness of Wolverhampton. Wolverhampton is well known for its rich history as a traditional industrial city that could make just about anything in its manufacturing heyday – from cars and motor cycles to world-renowned beers. It still retains this hard-working edge but its new city status is not just about marking the turn of the new millennium; it is a recognition that Wolverhampton has much more to offer and a broader role to play in the development of the West Midlands.

It is a city where manufacturing still accounts for 23 per cent of employment, but conversely it also acts as a major centre for culture, the arts, leisure and higher education, and the pace of change and renewal has helped to turn Wolverhampton into a young, thriving city, proud of its diversity and cultures and with strong sustainable communities. Investment in the city is at a real high and is taking place across a wide spectrum – from commerce and industry to housing, education and health, and Wolverhampton's future is secure with much more planned investment.

Those who live in, work in or simply visit Wolverhampton are often surprised at our quality of life. It's an exciting university city with a reputation for excellent night-time entertainment, and people are spoilt for choice in the many clubs and bars that attract thousands at the weekend. Of course, for those who prefer a more sedate pace, the city has an enviable range of restaurants, a famous Victorian theatre and a busy Civic Hall which brings leading entertainment into Wolverhampton. We have a good range of hotels, the regions third-ranked retail centre, Europe's first all-weather floodlit racecourse and we will, of course, always be known as the home of the famous Wanderers.

Over the years Wulfrunians have witnessed at first hand the changes that have transformed Wolverhampton, not least the significant improvements to the public transport network with our Metro system running into the heart of Birmingham every six minutes. Much more work is planned and major redevelopment projects in the city centre and Bilston will go a long way to satisfy our aspirations in modern homes and canal-side apartments.

During this special year we have been busy celebrating the Queen's Golden Jubilee, which has brought communities together and has given immense enjoyment to our citizens. Having just celebrated the millennium and its first official birthday, the newest city in the Midlands looks forward to a bright and prosperous future with enthusiasm and optimism.

Robert Hart
The Right Worshipful the Mayor of Wolverhampton, 2002–3

Wolverhampton Jubilee Civic Sunday, 16 June 2002, was an occasion that brought many different Wulfrunians together in all the most quintessential city locations: St Peter's Church, Lichfield Street, Queen Square and the Civic Centre. The civic Sunday parade has traditionally been led by local firefighters and their band. After the parade local firefighters lined up for a picture. Left to right: Mel Kinsey, Andy Fellows, Neil Kinsey, Gary Fellows, Keith Orchard, Kerrigan Bradley, Gordon Sambrook, Dave Smith and Tony Ball. *(Ned Williams)*

To clear the square for this event the local skateboarders had to vacate their usual patch – so, by default, they became part of the event as well! Skateboarders are more reluctant to be identified than firefighters, and two have hidden behind their boards. *(Ned Williams)*

Introduction

Wolverhampton spent the nineteenth and twentieth centuries growing and changing. As a result, most Wulfrunians have a view about the past and a view about the present. The Second World War and its aftermath seemed to provide a period when Wolverhampton stood still for a time. But the process of change and renewal began once more with a vengeance in the 1960s. This came as quite a shock to a generation of Wulfrunians who looked upon the past as something relatively static, and the new 'present' as a time of endless and unpleasant change. The moment which helped this generation chart the beginning of the 'decline and fall' of Wolverhampton is illustrated on page 15: in 1960 the market patch was moved from its central position between St Peter's Church and the Town Hall.

A book of photographs opens up the discussion all over again. Have things got worse? Have they got better? Has a golden age of Wolverhampton gone forever? Is it just beginning? What's happened to our industries? What have we done to our neighbours? Are we part of the Black Country? What does it mean to be a city? How do you qualify to call yourself a Wulfrunian? What is going on in Wolverhampton?

Photographs do not provide straightforward answers; they just provide lots of food for thought. Sometimes they remind us that some things have not changed as much as we thought. Sometimes they do the opposite. Change is a complicated business. Several of the city-centre street scenes reveal that some of Wolverhampton's vistas are remarkable for their general continuity rather than their change, and key locations like Queen Square and Lichfield Street have managed to be quite adaptable as well as enduring. Travelling away from the centre of the city, one comes to the ring road. This epic construction took twenty-five years to complete and has had a colossal effect on the city in many different respects. Beyond the ring road, areas like Blakenhall, Whitmore Reans, Graisley, Dunstall and Heath Town went though massive changes in the 1960s and continue to alter today. The outer suburbs have been more settled, but beyond them are new satellites like Pendeford and Perton – the latter technically not part of Wolverhampton at all.

Wolverhampton's industries diversified in the 1880s when the iron trades went through one of their periodic times of crisis. The town also attracted major new employers, in the form of Goodyear and Courtaulds in the 1920s, when many others faced industrial and economic difficulties. Wolverhampton also adapted to the loss of its own cycle and vehicle industries, which had seemed so important in the early years of the twentieth century. But, of course, it hung on to the manufacture of parts and components in both vehicle and aerospace engineering.

Despite all this, no town could escape the changes in industry that came from the 1970s onwards. Familiar company names disappeared; unemployment became a real

Wolverhampton has a special association with motorcycles. Sunbeam, AJS, Norton Villiers, HRD and Wolf are all names that link the city with motorcycle manufacture. In the twenty-first century the city boasts a Harley-Davidson dealership in Chapel Ash, not far from the sites of the factories where Wolverhampton's own bikes were built. In 2002 Beacon Radio FM's traffic reporter 'Porky' (Ian Jones) was given a Harley for his job. Left to right: Mark, 'Porky' and Jo, all presenters on Beacon Radio, pose outside the station in Tettenhall Road. (*Beacon Radio FM*)

problem and regeneration a new obsession. Town centres were faced by new challenges in the worlds of retailing and leisure. Congestion and transport became 'issues'.

But 'past and present' does not have to be seen only in terms of the physical environment. Every aspect of human life in Wolverhampton also changes – work, domestic life, education, religion, leisure and entertainment. Therefore, this book also tries briefly to survey such things via photographs.

There are two aspects of change that are difficult to illustrate in the time and space available. The first is Wolverhampton's journey towards becoming a 'city' – finally achieved in May 2001. The second is Wolverhampton's special character as a home to incomers. The business of coming to Wolverhampton, and sometimes deciding to put down some roots in the place, is not a process that is necessarily recorded in people's collections of photographs – it exists more clearly in their oral biographies. However, a chapter has been devoted to this theme because it definitely forms a positive part of the city's story of its own development.

Becoming a city and celebrating the millennium both seem to follow earlier milestone events – Wolverhampton's own millennium in 1985, and the millennium of St Peter's in 1994. Now, in 2002, we celebrate another anniversary: Queen Elizabeth's Golden Jubilee. All these birthdays are moments for looking back, looking forward, and contemplating change – hence this book.

Ned Williams
August 2002

The Wolverhampton Scene

St Peter's Church represents what is permanent about the man-made environment of Wolverhampton. The Market Place and Retail Market Hall, seen here in the mid-1950s, represent the ever-changing environment of the town. When the market moved early in 1960 it seemed to herald the current wave of change to which many Wulfrunians have never adjusted. *(Express & Star)*

Queen Square acquired its name after Queen Victoria's visit in 1866, and has long enjoyed its unofficial status as the 'town centre'. This late 1920s view of the square from Darlington Street features James Beattie's growing store on the right, the Hippodrome Theatre (1898–1956, and until 1921 known as the Empire) on the far side of North Street and the Queen's Cinema (1914–59) in the square. *(Ken Rock Collection)*

Just over seventy years later Queen Square still forms a natural city centre. The Hippodrome was replaced with a very functional building, but the recently erected frontage of Yates's Wine Lodge does greater justice to the location. The cinema has been lost in an extension to Lloyds Bank, and the square has become greener over the years. Beattie's finally acquired the former Burton's building (right), and completed its occupation of the land between Victoria Street and Darlington Street. *(Ned Williams)*

Lichfield Street was widened and improved in the 1880s as Victorian Wolverhampton prospered and expanded. Princes Square, halfway along its length, was another contender for the title of 'town centre'. The Royal London Building dominates the area in this Edwardian postcard view, taken before the arrival of Wolverhampton's pioneering set of traffic lights. *(Ken Rock Collection)*

The same view today reassures us that much of Wolverhampton's Victorian architectural heritage has survived in the city centre, but the Royal London Building is now owned by a large brewery and leisure group and much of the ground floor space is occupied by bars. The development of this area as a leisure and entertainment centre has been seen as one of the city's successes in recent years.
(Ned Williams)

The Wolverhampton Art Gallery was opened in 1885. Designed by Julius Chatwin, it was paid for by Mr Philip Horsman JP, a local builder. It formed a major contribution to the 1880s renewal of this part of the town, along with the memorial gardens laid out on the left and the fountain, which was unveiled in 1896. An art gallery was almost as important a feature for a Victorian town of any prestige as a clean water supply or a modern gasworks. *(Author's Collection)*

In 2002 Senior Art Gallery Curator Marguerite Nugent contemplates a model of the gallery's recent extensions and improvements, phase one of which was completed in 2001. The gallery has collected works of art for over one hundred years and now plans increased exhibition space and modern craft studios at the Wulfruna Street end of the building. *(Express & Star)*

Bilston Street has always been a busy gateway to the town's centre and this picture, taken in July 1980, shows many of the old buildings about to be swept away in the redevelopment of the street. The largest building was the Clifton Cinema, which had enjoyed a long and complex history with many changes of name. It opened as the Prince of Wales Theatre on 4 May 1863 and acquired the frontage seen here in 1914. It was demolished in 1982. *(Keith Hodgkins)*

Bilston Street today still forms a vital artery from the city centre to the ring road, and has become the terminus of the Midland Metro from Birmingham, opened on 31 May 1999. The new police station, occupying the left-hand side of the street, was opened in July 1992 by Diana, Princess of Wales. The Atlantis, a night-club, now occupies the former Savoy/ABC/Cannon Cinema, much rebuilt, on the right. *(Ned Williams)*

In May 1961 the town end of Bilston Street was still the terminus of the 58 trolleybus route from Dudley. This was the last trolleybus route to be withdrawn, closing in March 1967. (No. 497 seen here was a Park Royal-bodied Guy vehicle of 1949 vintage.) The Garrick's Head public house has an elegant 1930s feel to its design. Mac Fisheries occupies the old 'Kings Head' building. *(Clifford Brown, John Hughes Collection)*

Since the 1960s much of the city centre has been pedestrianised, with parking provided for disabled drivers. Bilston Street, photographed here in 1997, is now pedestrianised and tree-lined. The Birmingham Midshires Building Society has moved into the old Garrick's Head, retaining the style of the building's exterior. *(Ned Williams)*

Clarkson's Furniture Store on the corner of Snow Hill and Cleveland Street is keen to tell its customers that the business was established in 1840 in this John Price postcard produced before the First World War. Snow Hill led out to the Georgian suburb of Wolverhampton built around St John's Church, which itself dates back to 1760, reflecting the early expansion of Wolverhampton. *(John Masefield Collection)*

A furniture store still trades on the corner of Snow Hill today, in a steel-framed 1930s structure. Beyond it the nineteenth-century buildings have been replaced with a 1960s property first occupied by Rackams as a department store; it now houses a Netto supermarket with the city's archives above. Beyond Temple Street, the very old buildings facing Snow Hill have recently undergone massive restoration, and this regeneration work is now extending to the area around St John's Church. *(Ned Williams)*

The junction of Stafford Street and Broad Street provides a good view of the George Hotel on the corner of Wulfruna Street – a 1930s building on the site of a former public house of the same name. The Technical College of 1932 and the National Foundry College were also developed during the 1930s. *(The Robinson Collection)*

Reflecting the fact that the town's Technical College has grown into the city's university, the George has become the Varsity. Trolleybuses no longer negotiate the roundabout to reach Stafford Street, but note the colourful flowerbeds that now fill the centre of Princes Street. *(Ned Williams)*

The new Retail Market was hailed as a major success in the restyling of parts of Wolverhampton in the 1960s, and in relocating the town's market itself. It was opened by Lord Morrison of Lambeth on 22 June 1960. This picture of the entrance to the indoor market was taken soon after the opening, and gives prominence to the subway beneath School Street – a fashionable way of separating pedestrians and traffic. *(Bill Bawden)*

The revamped entrance to the Retail Market photographed in 2002 illustrates the need for the remodelling of some 1960s contributions to the townscape, and shows how the open market is now relocated along a pedestrianised School Street. Further redevelopment will lead to the building of a new city square on the site between the market and Worcester Street. This will also bring new housing into the central area. *(Ned Williams)*

When the Queen's Cinema opened in 1914 the building included a fashionable tea-room on the balcony, seen here in a contemporary photograph in all its oak-panelled glory. Tea-rooms and restaurants such as Lyons Tea-Room and Reynolds Restaurant flourished in the central area around Queen Square. *(Author's Collection)*

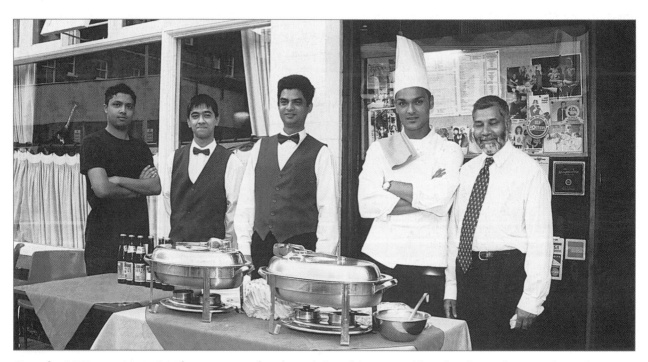

Since the 1950s catering in British town centres has diversified, and 'eating out' has played a vital part in the city's current emphasis on developing leisure and entertainment. The staff of the Dilshad Indian Restaurant in Berry Street take up position outside the restaurant on 22 June 2002 to take part in a street party to mark the opening of the 'artists' quarter' in Berry Street and Princes Alley. Right to left: Mr M. Uddin, the proprietor for the last thirty-five years, Mukul Choudhury (chef), Lippon Khan (head waiter), Syed Shaid and Kamal Ali (waiters). *(Ned Williams)*

This 1930s picture of J. Whilton's premises on the Dudley Road shows meat arriving 'on the hoof' from the Cleveland Road market. Even in the town centre butchers slaughtered on the premises and prepared their own meat for the customers. The introduction of freezers, pre-packed meat and new shopping habits have changed all this. *(Eardley Lewis Collection)*

Supermarkets, and now out-of-town hypermarkets, reflect some of the changes that have taken place in the world of retailing. The Safeway superstore at Pendeford was opened on 3 December 1985. Like the Sainsbury's, opened at Perton on 8 September 1981, this store can make journeys to the city centre unnecessary. Closer to the centre itself large stores have opened in a circle just outside the ring road in a trend that was started by Asda in the mid-1980s in a building just behind the Wolves ground. *(Author's Collection)*

Chapel Ash was a thriving 'gateway' commercial centre until the building of the ring road began to consign it to twilight status from the mid-1960s onwards. In this Edwardian John Price postcard view Chapel Ash is busy, although the new electric trams provide the only sign of traffic. Charles Clarke's garage on the corner of Bath Road is the only indication that we are entering the motor age. *(Ken Rock Collection)*

Chapel Ash today. The built environment has changed little, although traffic often now chokes this artery into the city. Double yellow lines rule and retailing is dominated by estate agents and food take-aways of all types. The tree outside the Combermere Arms has grown a little, and the spire of St Mark's Church conceals the fact that the building itself has had to find a new use. It has been converted into prestigious office accommodation currently used by financial consultants. *(Ned Williams)*

The Davenport's Beer delivery man has abandoned his dray outside 474 Cannock Road one afternoon in 1929 to have a cup of tea with the new tenants. The 21-year-old girl giving the horse a drink was Olive Jones, who died in January 2002 at the age of ninety-four, and the family have just returned the tenancy of no. 474 to the council after ninety-three years! In 1929 the other side of the road looked out over fields and massive suburban development was yet to take place. *(Terry Hickman)*

The view from 474 Cannock Road today. The Golden Lion was built in the 1930s, as the suburbs expanded through Fallings Park and along the Cannock Road. To the right on the far side of Old Fallings Lane, Somerfield now has a supermarket where the Clifton Cinema briefly existed between 1940 and 1960. *(Ned Williams)*

In the 1900s 'oatmeal and water' was always ready for those Wulfrunians able to make the horse-drawn journey out along the Cannock road to the corner of Peartree Lane. George Thomas Boult and his wife stand in the doorway of the Peartree Inn. Later the pub was run by Bert Adey who promoted boxing in the grounds at the back. *(Reg Garrington)*

In the 1930s the Peartree Inn was rebuilt and today it is named the Mill House, but of course it still stands at the corner of Peartree Lane. The photograph is taken from what looks like a lay-by on the Cannock road. This is is really the only remaining evidence of the turning circle provided for the 13 trolleybus route that was opened to this point in March 1932 – reflecting the town's suburban growth at the time. *(Ned Williams)*

At the opposite end of Wolverhampton, suburban sprawl spread through Compton, Finchfield and Penn in the 1930s when the town took over territory that had formerly been part of the Rural District of Siesdon. In this John Price postcard of the 1900s the Mermaid Inn stands by the empty crossroads at Wightwick. *(Ken Rock Collection)*

Today this junction has become busy enough to demand traffic lights but the Mermaid still looks very rural. The old turnpike road to Bridgnorth now carries commuters to and from Perton, the huge housing development in South Staffordshire just beyond Wolverhampton's border. Behind the Mermaid is Wightwick Manor, formerly one of the homes of the Mander family, and now in the hands of the National Trust. *(Ned Williams)*

From the mid-nineteenth century onwards Wolverhampton acquired a distinctive suburb in the form of Whitmore Reans. This community was fairly self-contained and provided for all human needs ranging from churches to cinemas. One of the many pubs in the district was the Round House, seen here in 1961. It stood on the corner of Coleman Street and Gatis Street, close to St Andrew's Church and the West End Cinema, later known as the Rex. *(Dave Whyley Collection)*

This area was so altered in the 1960s that many locations are now unrecognisable. The modern hexagonal library stands close to the original junction of Coleman Street and Gatis Street, just behind the Avion Centre, seen here on the left, which continues to provide Whitmore Reans with local shopping facilities. *(Ned Williams)*

Like Whitmore Reans and Blakenhall, Heath Town was another of Wolverhampton's inner suburbs that underwent huge changes in the 1960s. Numerous well-known pubs disappeared in these redevelopments. The Travellers Rest was photographed in 1947 when it stood on the main road. Note the advert for the Olympia Cinema, at that time still operating in Thornley Street. *(Dave Whyley Collection)*

The old Travellers Rest disappeared in the 1960s as the Wednesfield road was widened. Heath Town's massive redevelopment included the tower blocks seen here, opened by Princess Margaret in April 1969. The new Travellers Rest was built well back from the main road. After a chequered career it was eventually closed. The pub's name has now found new meaning, however, inasmuch as the building is now a day centre for the elderly. *(Ned Williams)*

The Lord Raglan, on the corner of Raglan Street and Brick Kiln Street, was another nineteenth-century building that was replaced in the 1960s. The three-storey Georgian-style building seen here reflects the mid-nineteenth-century expansion of Wolverhampton into the area of Graisley, now divided from the city centre by the ring road. *(Eileen Beards Collection)*

The new Lord Raglan prospered under its famous local landlord, the musician Tommy Burton, but it has since fallen on hard times. It now stands boarded up awaiting a decision on proposals for the major redevelopment of this area, pending a planning application for a new Sainsbury's superstore. *(Ned Williams)*

Penn Fields is a fascinating residential area featuring housing from different decades. Jeffcock Road, seen here in a 1930s postcard, includes housing of the Edwardian era and the inter-war period. No. 224 on the left has just been built and the trees have yet to mature. *(Barry Tranter Collection)*

A present-day view of the same section of Jeffcock Road shows some growth in the trees and some 'infilling' – for example a relatively modern house has appeared between no. 224 and the neighbouring bungalow. The distinctive garden wall on the right still exists. Like all such streets, Jeffcock Road is now clogged up with parked cars. *(Ned Williams)*

Industrial streetscapes have often changed considerably, but some remain stubbornly recognisable. Here a post-war Sunbeam trolleybus (no. 454) glides along Park Lane in about 1960, passing the Park Lane Corporation Transport Depot on the right. On the left is the factory belonging to Guy Motors, also associated with trolleybus manufacture. *(Phil Lycett)*

Trolleybus wires no longer fill the sky above Park Lane but the Travel West Midlands Depot is to be seen, together with that curious little building on the extreme right which is next to the Paget Arms. Housing and an industrial estate can be seen on the left but some of the Guy Motors building still stands, carrying a blue plaque commemorating the firm's existence. The bus is an Optare L1070 of 1999 vintage. *(Ned Williams)*

The Happiest Days of Your Life

Mrs Cunliffe and her class at St Andrew's C of E Junior School, Whitmore Reans, 1968. The picture was taken on the site of what is now the Farndale School. In 1978 St Andrew's moved to the building formerly used by the Whitmore School in Coleman Street. No wonder everyone is confused! *(Maria Maragliano Collection)*

Starting young: children pose for the camera at Holy Trinity Infants' School, Ettingshall, some time before the First World War. Every child looks well-shod and well turned-out but everyone looks very solemn. *(Ken Rock Collection)*

As little as fifty years ago the only groups catering for children's needs outside school were Sunday schools and uniformed organisations. Since that time the importance of nursery education, pre-school playgroups, mother and toddler groups and the like has been recognised. Here are members of the Peach Tree Community Association waiting to join the parade on Civic Sunday, 16 June 2002. Led by Noreen Turner MBE (second from right in the back row), the volunteer adults seen here run after-school clubs and playgroups for the children of Low Hill. *(Ned Williams)*

Two children at Stow
Heath Junior School in
the mid-1950s pose
beside their model of an
Eskimo village. The boy is
wearing jumper, shirt
and tie, short trousers
and school socks – school
fashion of the day. The
class hamster's cage
seems to be on the right
of the picture. *(Stow
Heath Primary School
Archive)*

At the same school today
pupils are dressed in
modern uniform and seem
to take working with new
technology for granted.
The wall charts are
professionally presented
and illustrate the use of
computer graphics. These
children are more likely to
construct a website than
an Eskimo village. *(Stow
Heath Primary School
Archive)*

The girls' rounders team at Bushbury Hill Junior School in 1958. In those days they were Fourth Year pupils, about to leave for the world of secondary education. Today they are Year Six pupils and barely have time for rounders due to the demands of basic literacy, basic numeracy and the national curriculum. *(Sheila Edwards)*

In 2002 the girls are just as likely to be interested in football as the lads – and so what we see here is the Stow Heath Primary School girls' football team. There seem to be a lot more smiles around than in earlier school photos. *(Stow Heath Primary School Archive)*

Girls aged between five and sixteen at Ely House School, Tettenhall Road, in 1948. The two boys in the picture belong to the kindergarten. Mrs Shaw, the headmistress, is in the centre of the picture, sitting next to another Mrs Shaw, the sports mistress. Uniforms were navy blue, with a royal blue stripe in the hat-bands. *(Audrey Evans)*

In April 2002 a reunion of former Ely House girls was organised, and a number of them were photographed here outside the school premises – now a restaurant and hotel. The three girls holding the 'Next Term Commences' board are Penny Whitehouse (née Chapman), Betty Ward (née Allerton) and Pauline Gee (née Hood). Hats, scarves and blazers were found for the occasion. *(Express & Star)*

The Higher Grade Secondary Day School was built in 1894 and opened the following year to extend the level of education then available at local board schools. When education was 'municipalised' in 1902 the school began its journey towards becoming the Municipal Grammar School. This postcard view of the school in Edwardian times shows New Hampton Road empty of traffic although the tram tracks, opened in 1902, are clearly visible. Campion's shop on the corner of Dunkley Street appears in many pictures. *(Ken Rock Collection)*

Best known as the Municipal Grammar School, it went through many name changes on its way to the twenty-first century, although the building's exterior has changed very little. It is now the New Hampton Centre, shared by the City of Wolverhampton College and its partners. *(Ned Williams)*

The World of Work

The Electric Construction Company's Bushbury Engineering Works decorated for the Coronation in 1953. The ECC brought electrical engineering to Wolverhampton when the town's industries were diversifying at the end of the nineteenth century. Its large workforce and very visible premises seemed to be an essential part of Wolverhampton but, like many other manufacturers who were household names, it has now vanished from the landscape. *(Author's Collection)*

The core-making shop at the Electric Construction Company brought the traditional metal-working skills of Wolverhampton into the orbit of the electrical engineering industry. In the early 1960s when this picture was taken there were still many foundries in Wolverhampton, but they too have all vanished. *(Author's Collection)*

The Goodyear tyre factory came to Wolverhampton in 1927 and today its site between Stafford Road and Bushbury Lane still provides one of Wolverhampton's few genuinely industrial skylines – but for how much longer? *(Ned Williams)*

Moorfield Road was at the heart of industrial Blakenhall in the 1940s. This building had been part of the Sunbeam Works but was then being used by Turner Manufacturing. *(Eardley Lewis Collection)*

Moorfield Road today runs through the centre of the IMEX complex. The old industrial buildings have been given a reprieve by being turned into many small separate units in a vast warren of activity. On the skyline are the high-rise Blakenhall flats, which transformed the area when they were built in the 1960s. *(Ned Williams)*

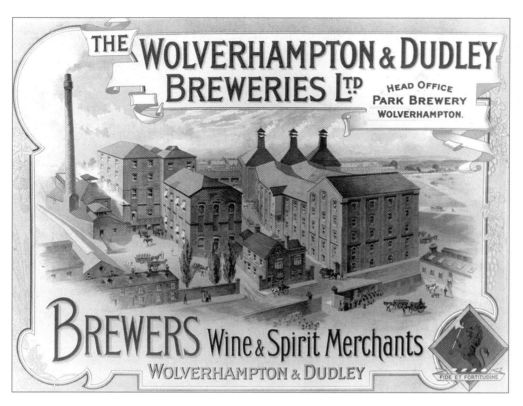

The Park Brewery at Chapel Ash belongs to the Wolverhampton & Dudley Breweries Ltd, but everyone knows the institution simply as 'Banks's'. The company was established in 1890 by amalgamating a number of South Staffordshire brewing and malting concerns. The new brewery was built soon after that date along modern lines. As can be seen from the illustration on this 1900s advertisement, the site included maltings. (*Author's Collection*)

Members of the Thompson family were among the directors of the Wolverhampton & Dudley Breweries in the 1890s and the family is still represented in the firm today. The brewery site still occupies a large area between Chapel Ash, Meadow Street, Bath Road, the ring road and Lovatt Street, and it is almost impossible to take it all in from one location. (*Ned Williams*)

The famous Wolverhampton firm of Mander Brothers was formed in 1753 by Benjamin and John Mander. It manufactured varnish which tied in with the town's 'japanning' trade in which papier mâché products were finished in a varnish or enamel before being baked. From its town centre location Mander Brothers moved out to Heath Town, where the paint warehouse was photographed in the 1960s. (*Author's Collection*)

Separated by a canal and the railway track from the old site of the Manders paint factory was the large abandoned railway goods yard adjacent to the Wednesfield Road. The large Midland Railway grain warehouse on the site was considered worthy of conservation but such was the pressure to bring new jobs to Wolverhampton in the 1990s that the building was demolished overnight in August 1997 to make way for a massive Post Office sorting office, which opened on 27 November 1998. A large Parcelforce articulated lorry pulls away from the new mail centre in July 2002. It has brought new jobs to the city, changed the landscape and even invented a new region: 'the North West Midlands'. (*Ned Williams*)

Irene Frost and Iris Green at the Wolverhampton Fire & Ambulance Service Control Centre at the Merridale Street fire station in 1973. Emergency services have been provided on a county-wide basis since 1974 and calls to the West Midlands Fire Service today are dealt with centrally in Birmingham. *(Mel Kinsey Collection)*

The former control room in the fire station in Merridale Street is now a general office furnished with the customary computer, keyboard, printer and so on. *(Kevin Cartwright)*

Kathleen Reed became Low Hill's first ARP warden in November 1941 at the age of sixteen. (She should have been eighteen to qualify for service!) At first she was issued nothing but an overall and a tin hat, but later received a uniform which she is wearing in this photograph taken at the back of 111 First Avenue (later demolished). *(Kathleen Burns Collection)*

There is now considerable nostalgia surrounding the world of the Home Guard ('Dad's Army') and wartime institutions like ARP wardens and the Auxiliary Fire Service. Kevin Cartwright, a Wolverhampton firefighter, takes this 1942 National Fire Service Austin towing vehicle and Dennis trailer pump to rallies. He is wearing NFS uniform of the period. *(Ned Williams)*

As in many other towns, employment has increasingly been found in the service and finance sectors. In May 1955 two cashiers working for the Wolverhampton Co-operative Society, Maisie Kearns and Marjorie Bowman, show signs of hysteria as Dividend Week approaches. The cashiers would be going on tour to several branch stores where members would collect their 'divi' payments. *(Marjorie Bowman Collection)*

Cashiers today are called 'Customer Advisors', and Yvonne Williams and Anita Webb of the Staffordshire Building Society dress to present a corporate image. The advertisement on the wall uses a Staffordshire Terrier to promote the Society in a manner that stresses local identity. While banks have become more global, several local building societies have preserved their mutuality and local identity. The picture also shows a modern low counter designed for use by customers in wheelchairs – something that nobody had thought of when Marjorie and Maisie were paying out the 'divi' in 1955. *(Staffordshire Building Society)*

Retailing is a major part of the service sector and it has seen many changes in the twentieth century. On 29 November 1958 staff and customers were photographed as they grappled with the new concept of 'self-service' at the Pendeford Lane Branch of the Wolverhampton Co-operative Society! They are being watched by officials from Head Office, who are probably wondering where all this is going to lead. *(Cynthia Stuart Collection)*

Since those far-off revolutionary days retailing has gone through many other changes. Supermarkets have been replaced by hypermarkets, while the concept of 'open all hours' has been reinvented in the 'convenience store'. Twenty-four-hour shopping has been brought to Wolverhampton, and Christmas Day opening has followed Sunday opening. The picture shows the present face of the Pendeford Lane Branch of what is now the West Midlands Co-operative Society. *(Ned Williams)*

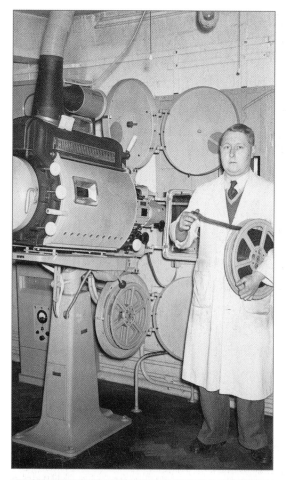

Eric Turvey was a projectionist at the Penn Cinema from 1937 to 1973, and he is seen here, in the late 1960s, next to the Philips projector that was pioneered there. The chief projectionist at the Penn, Cyril Moore, projected both the first and the last films screened at the cinema. A Somerfield supermarket now stands on the site. *(Eric Turvey Collection)*

In May 2002 the projection room at the city's Light House Cinema seems more cluttered as operator Richard Terry stands alongside the single machine that is about to show the whole programme – without reel changes – with the film wound on to the 'cakestand' seen on the extreme left of the picture. *(Ned Williams)*

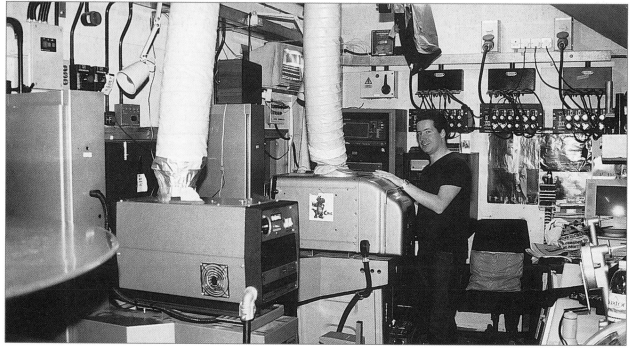

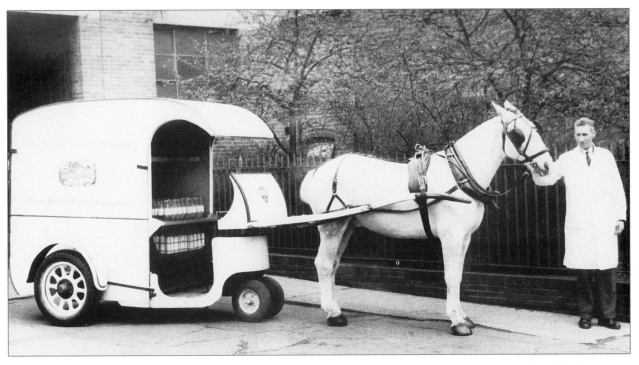

A milkman poses alongside the latest streamlined milk float introduced to Wolverhampton in the 1950s by Midland Counties Dairy, based on Penn Road. Several companies in Wolverhampton produced milk floats, including Sunbeam and Graisley. *(Author's Collection)*

Keith Fletcher stands alongside his electric milk float in 2002. He has been a milkman in Wolverhampton for forty-one years. He started work for Midland Counties Dairy, but now operates a franchise from Express Dairies. *(Ned Williams)*

The workers have to be fed: this 1937 picture of a tea trolley was taken at Sankey's Bankfield Works. Ruth Brown, on the left, was a press worker released from her post a couple of times a day to take round tea and biscuits. *(Ruth Brown Collection)*

With the closure of large factories the works canteen has become an endangered species. The mobile canteen has found a new home on industrial estates to provide this essential service. Here, in 2002, John Aston serves a grateful customer from his pitch near the old Villiers factory in Marston Road. *(Ned Williams)*

Wolverhampton Churches

On Friday 24 June 1994 Queen Elizabeth II visited St Peter's Collegiate Church in Wolverhampton to join the celebrations for the church's millennium. Here she is being escorted into the church by the rector, John Hall Matthewman, and greeted by local schoolchildren. *(Robert Shone)*

St Peter's Church stands in the centre of Wolverhampton at the top of the hill on which the settlement grew. Its long history is closely interwoven with that of the town, and it was naturally one of the first subjects for early photography. This particular picture appears to be part of a set, taken in the 1870s, before Lichfield Street was modernised in the 1880s, and well before the churchyard area was laid out as ornamental memorial gardens. This process was not completed until the mid-1890s. *(St Peter's Church Collection)*

The gardens between St Peter's Church and Lichfield Street considerably enhance the city centre and have been the subject of several refurbishments. The fountain of 1896 is a memorial to Philip Horsman, who provided Wolverhampton with the adjoining Art Gallery. The sailor's bust is a memorial to Douglas Harris, Wolverhampton's naval hero of the First World War. *(Ned Williams)*

St Peter's Collegiate Church has enjoyed a musical tradition stretching back over five hundred years, and it is one of the few churches in the city still to use a male-voice choir at its regular Sunday services. The choir is seen here outside the church in the 1950s. *(St Peter's Church Collection)*

St Peter's Collegiate Church choir and choirmaster in the twenty-first century. *(St Peter's Church Collection)*

The choir at St Peter's Church provides musical training not available elsewhere in Wolverhampton, and is now supported by The Friends of the Music of St Peter's Collegiate Church. It is hoped that this renewed interest in music at the church will lead to the restoration of the organ. *(Regent Records/Abbey Studios)*

A girls' choir was formed at St Peter's in 1999 to sing at choral services on weekdays, and to join the male-voice choir at major festivals. The girls are seen here in an informal pose inside the church. Both choirs take cathedral tours and have now made a CD of their work. *(Regent Records/Abbey Studios)*

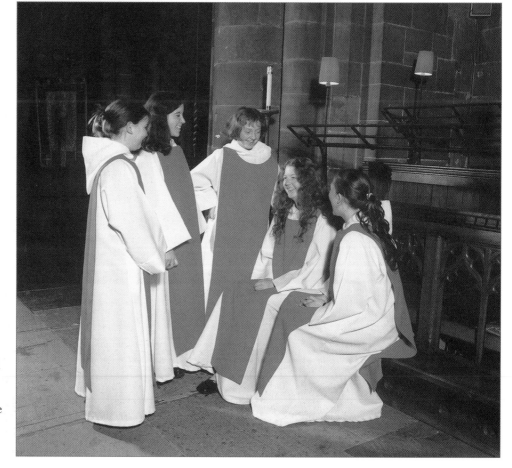

The Nonconformist churches have maintained a strong presence in Wolverhampton. Everyone is aware of the large Methodist Church in Darlington Street and its place in the local townscape. Its presence seems so solid that it is difficult to imagine that it ever looked any different. John Wesley opened the first Methodist Chapel in Wolverhampton in 1787. This church was built in 1825, soon after the setting out of Darlington Street, and was enlarged in 1859, when the tower was added. *(Eardley Lewis Collection)*

The present incarnation of the Darlington Street Methodist Church retains only the tower of its predecessor, but it still dominates the lower end of Darlington Street and the western approach to the city centre. It has recently celebrated its centenary. The foundation stone was laid in 1900 by Sir Henry Fowler, later Lord Wolverhampton, and the £19,000 building was opened on 29 October 1901. Many notable Wulfrunians were associated with this church. *(Ned Williams)*

In October 1980 the church's first Afro-Caribbean Evening was organised by Silbert Griffiths (on the left, next to his wife Doris). The evening raised £400 towards the church's £30,000 Refurbishment Fund. The Darlington Street church had a long history of welcoming newcomers to Wolverhampton and in the late 1950s held 'International Services' once a month. Even so, newcomers often felt it took a long time to be accepted as equals within the church. (*Doris Griffiths Collection*)

The minister, the Revd Tony Kinch, is seen in Darlington Street Methodist Church with the cast of the nativity play in 2001. (*Darlington Street Methodist Church Collection*)

In the early 1900s there were 17 Church of England churches (including 'missions'), 33 Nonconformist meeting places and 4 Roman Catholic churches in Wolverhampton. An event often photographed in the Roman Catholic churches was first communion, and here we see the first communicants lined up at St Mary's & St John's in May 1956. *(Kathleen Quirke Collection)*

Father Emmanuel and the first communicants line up for a photograph in St Mary's and St John's Church, Snow Hill, on 26 May 2002 – before dashing off to a communion breakfast in the Church Hall. The boys wear red sashes and ties over white shirts and the girls wear white dresses and veils. Construction of this church began in 1855. *(Ned Williams)*

The Roman Catholic churches became a religious and social centre in the lives of many of Wolverhampton's newcomers, some of whom moved on to create their own facilities. The first communicants of the Polish congregation at St Patrick's Church are seen here in the 1960s. *(Jan Glogowski)*

In the 1990s the first communicants in the Polish Roman Catholic congregation are able to take communion in their own church built on the Stafford Road and completed in the 1970s. They are seen here with Father W. Jarecki, the first priest at this church. *(Jan Glogowski)*

St Patrick's Church, Westbury Street and Littles Lane, photographed in the 1960s before the building was demolished to make way for the advance of the ring road. The church was built in 1867 and it was well sited to serve the Irish population of Wolverhampton who settled in the area between Stafford Road and Broad Street. Its replacement now stands in Heath Town. *(Jan Glogowski)*

The Polish Catholics who had used St Peter's and St Paul's and St Patrick's Church in the 1950s and 1960s established their own church on Stafford Road. *(Jan Glogowski)*

The first Kingdom Hall in Wolverhampton was established by the Jehovah's Witnesses in 1955 with a congregation of about eighty who came from far afield. It was simply an upper room in premises in Clarence Street, Chapel Ash. This photograph was taken at the wedding of Les and Isabel Wood who were married in a Kingdom Hall fashioned from a converted shop in St Johns Street on 24 July 1955. *(Bob Harrison)*

Today there are five new Kingdom Halls in Wolverhampton used by twelve congregations, involving over a thousand Wulfrunians. This hall in Parkfields, photographed on 21 July 2002, is used by three congregations. Les and Isabel, approaching their 47th wedding anniversary, are among the congregation! *(Ned Williams)*

The Salvation Army was well established in Wolverhampton at the end of the nineteenth century when it met in Dartmouth Street. A proper citadel was built in Cleveland Street next door to the Central Library. The band was photographed in this citadel in about 1966. The bandmaster is Charlie Handwell (centre), flanked by Lieutenants Mr and Mrs Turner, who led the Corps. *(Jean Head Collection)*

Local Salvationists today photographed at the Jubilee Year Civic Sunday Parade on 16 June 2002. Left to right: Jean Head, John Head, Captain Geoff Bonser, Peter Armstrong, Captain Glenys Bonser, June Armstrong and her grandson Lee. The Corps now meets at Eastfield in premises on the Willenhall Road. *(Ned Williams)*

Members of the Home League run by the Salvation Army in their citadel in Cleveland Road stand for a photograph in 1973. Captain and Mrs Malpass receive a shield for the best-attended Home League in the division. *(Jean Head Collection)*

The exterior of the Salvation Army Citadel in Cleveland Road. *c.* 1974. Note the separate entrance to the gallery on the side of the building. *(Ned Williams)*

The Salvation Army Citadel in Cleveland Road has become the Bethel Chapel and is now home to members of the African Methodist Episcopal Zion Church, led by their pastor, Lurleen Gooden. The pastor stands behind the lectern on the platform once occupied by the Salvation Army band and songsters. She is surrounded by the congregation in July 2002. *(Ned Williams)*

A female-voice choir takes the floor during a service at the Bethel Chapel in July 2002, and the congregation sit where the members of the Home League were standing in the picture opposite. *(Ned Williams)*

Many of Wolverhampton's Victorian church buildings have disappeared as congregations have declined or moved. Others have disappeared under developments like the ring road. St Mary's Church in Stafford Street was consecrated on 15 October 1842 and demolished in the 1960s. Its congregation was absorbed into St Peter's. *(St Peter's Church Collection)*

Some congregations have built new churches. Here, in July 2002, some of the congregation of the Italian Pentecostal Church in Gorsebrook Road stand outside their corrugated iron building which they acquired second-hand from the Church of England. Plans have been drawn up to replace this with a new modern structure on the same site. Fans of corrugated iron buildings will be sad to see yet another example disappear! *(Ned Williams)*

Wolverhampton on Wheels

Wolverhampton was definitely a 'town on wheels', with manufacturers of every kind of wheeled transport from bicycles to railway locomotives. The town also operated its own municipal public transport. Here Bernard Cooney proudly displays the uniform of a Wolverhampton Corporation Transport bus conductor – a well-known figure on the Compton route in the 1940s. *(Author's Collection)*

Not all passenger-carrying road services in Wolverhampton were operated by the Corporation. The Great Western Railway introduced a bus service from Wolverhampton Low Level station to Bridgnorth on 7 November 1904 using steam-powered vehicles, replaced the following year with petrol vehicles like this one. Here the GWR Road Traffic staff line up in 1924 at the Low Level station. *(Stan Webb Collection)*

In July 2002 an inspector and bus drivers employed by Travel West Midlands pause in their work at Wolverhampton's busy bus station. At its busiest time nearly two hundred buses pass through the station in an hour. *(Ned Williams)*

Wulfrunians were justifiably proud of their local municipal transport and the livery of apple green and primrose yellow still stirs the heart of every Wulfrunian over forty. Heads turn when Travel West Midland's bus no. 2989 wearing the old livery strides through the city. Here in 1960 WCT no. 585 (a Guy Arab IV with a Guy-built body) gleams as it waits outside the Cleveland Street Depot. The Corporation Transport operation was taken over by the West Midlands PTE in 1969, and the depot itself was rebuilt in 1978. *(Bill Bawden)*

In 2002 Travel West Midlands painted two Dennis Trident (Alexander-bodied) buses in a gold and purple livery to mark the Queen's Golden Jubilee. No. 4128 is seen here in July 2002 departing from Wolverhampton bus station on the 529 service to Walsall. *(Ned Williams)*

Wolverhampton was once an important railway town, and here, on 11 May 1958, ex-GWR 4–6–0 no. 5022 *Wigmore Castle* passes Stafford Road Junction with a Paddington–Birkenhead train. The tracks lead from the junction to Victoria Basin, passing through Stafford Road Works, where locomotives were built and then maintained until the works closed in 1964. *(Michael Hale)*

On 9 June 2002 ex-GWR pannier tank no. 7760 hauled a special train from Tyseley to Cosford air show. It is shown here on the approach to Stafford Road Junction, the photographer standing about where the signal was in the previous picture. All sign of the railway works has disappeared and a trading estate now stands on the left-hand part of the site. The train has reached this line via the High Level station – something that was impossible until a connection was installed in 1966 between the High Level line and the old Victoria Basin line. *(Ned Williams)*

Wulfrunian Ken Southern, sporting the new British Rail uniform of the day, takes the controls of a Brush class 47 diesel locomotive in September 1971. Ken had acquired some experience of working diesel locomotives while in the Army and as a local footplateman he took a key role in training Wolverhampton men for work on the new locomotives as steam was phased out. *(John Tranter/Ken Southern Collection)*

On 28 June 2002 a Virgin Trains driver and train manager walk back along Platform 3 at Wolverhampton, having just handed the train over to the crew taking it to London. Both wear Virgin Trains uniform, and the train manager's jacket is in a very distinctive bright red. Various train operating companies now serve Wolverhampton, each in their distinctive corporate colours. *(Wilf & Suzie Smith)*

The Mayor of Wolverhampton, Councillor Chris Laws, hands R. Chapman (Station Manager) a certificate after Wolverhampton High Level won the Regional Best Kept Station Award in 1984. Ken Southern, fourth from left, was the station supervisor who had instigated the clean-up. Staff wear 'Rail Blue' British Rail uniforms, and the Area Manager (Mr Carrit) wears a bowler hat. *(Ken Southern Collection)*

Today Virgin Railways staff wear bright red uniforms when dispatching trains and serving 'customers' (not 'passengers') at Wolverhampton station. Here electric locomotive no. 87011 was about to be named *City of Wolverhampton* on 5 February 2001. *(Ned Williams)*

Ex-LNER Pacific *Flying Scotsman* has had little to do with Wolverhampton but has paid the occasional visit. On 20 April 1963 she made her first public appearance since restoration in preservation on a Festiniog Railway Society special from Paddington to Ruabon. She was photographed coming through Wolverhampton Low Level from the Culwick Street bridge in a downpour. *(Bob Webster)*

On 7 October 1999 the *Flying Scotsman*, several owners later, reappeared in Wolverhampton on a special train to Chester. She is seen here crossing Oxley Viaduct, heading for Shrewsbury, passing above the rooftops of the new houses built at this extremity of the racecourse site. *(Ned Williams)*

On 6 February 1902 Wolverhampton Corporation (Tramways Department) ran its first electric trams up and down Cleveland Road between the new depot, seen in the background, and the junction with the Ettingshall Road. This was all very new and experimental, and the trams were fitted with Providence Lifeguards in raised and lowered positions, although these were abandoned once further services were introduced. *(Author's Collection)*

On 14 September 1999 the Princess Royal stepped from a tram on the Midland Metro at Bilston Street, Wolverhampton, to open the line officially. The photographer had patiently waited in this position for over an hour in order to capture the moment – but official guests were lined up across everybody's line of vision a few moments before the Princess arrived! *(Kiran Williams)*

Midland Red was another operator serving Wolverhampton. They were famous for building their own buses, but this vehicle was totally a Wolverhampton product. No. 3576, of 1949 vintage, was a Guy Arab bus with a Guy-built body, built under licence from Park Royal. The engine was built by Henry Meadows in Park Village. It was photographed outside the Salvation Army Citadel in Cleveland Road in April 1962. (*Simon Dewey*)

In May 2002 a Midland Red D9, restored by Roger Burdett and now in preservation, made a return visit to Wolverhampton and posed on the forecourt of the former Midland Red garage on Dudley Road. Originally fleet no. 5424, it was built in 1966 and withdrawn in 1977. The garage was opened in 1964, replacing one in Bilston Street, and closed on 1 October 1971. (*John James*)

This Wolverhampton-built Sunbeam, photographed in about 1908, belonged to the Fellows family who lived on the Bilston Road where they ran a sheet metal and galvanising works. (*Audrey Evans Collection*)

Today the annual Sunbeam owners' rallies attract Sunbeam drivers from far and wide. Here, on 4 July 1999, the drivers and cars have just assembled in the car park at the back of the former Sunbeam Works in Blakenhall, after driving across Wolverhampton from the Marston Factory on Wobaston Road. The IMEX industrial estate forms the background to this picture. (*Ned Williams*)

Here are the Wulfrunians

Joe Davies, wearing the PC39 uniform he first wore when he joined the Wolverhampton Borough Police in 1946. Since his retirement from the police, Joe has been one of Wolverhampton's unofficial ambassadors with his fairground organ *Lady Wulfrun*. Here he is taking care of the Kingscourt Dancers at the Wolverhampton Historic Vehicle Rally in West Park in June 2001. *(Ned Williams)*

The Mayor of the Borough of Wolverhampton in 1901–2 was Councillor Charles Paulton Plant JP from the Bilston family of brewers. After completing his education he 'dropped out' for a year or two and 'roughed it' in Australia and New Zealand before returning to the family firm. Some time later, when in control of Plants Brewery, he sold out to William Butler Ltd of Wolverhampton, whom he joined as a director. He entered local politics in 1896. During his year of office he opened the new electric tramways, hosted the Duke of Connaught at the opening of the Wolverhampton Industrial Exhibition in May 1902 and opened the new Free Library at Snow Hill. He lived in Richmond Road. (Ian Bott Collection)

The Mayor of the City of Wolverhampton in 2001–2 was Councillor Mrs Joyce Hill, supported by her granddaughter Victoria Griffiths as her mayoress. (It was the first time that a mayor's granddaughter had filled this role.) Joyce Hill worked for thirty-nine years as a nursing auxiliary at New Cross Hospital where she was an active trades unionist, and she first became a councillor in 1986 for the Fallings Park Ward. She has always lived in Wednesfield. (Wolverhampton City Council)

For many years
Wolverhampton's mayor
has hosted an annual civic
parade and church service.
In May 1927 Mayor Albert
Edward Wood descends the
steps of St Peter's Church
after the service, led by the
official mace-bearer and
followed by the Town Clerk,
Frederick Edwin Warbreck
Howell, and the Rector of
St Peter's Collegiate Church.
(P. Eisenhofer)

On Sunday 16 June 2002
the Mayor of the City of
Wolverhampton, Councillor
Robert Hart, descends the
steps of St Peter's after the
Jubilee Civic Service. He is
preceded by the official
Mace-bearer, Ann Hodson.
and followed by the Chief
Executive of the City
Council, Derrick Anderson.
(Ned Williams)

Members of the Royal Antediluvian Order of the Buffalo, Provident Lodge, seen in the 1920s at one of their meetings at the Lewisham Arms in Prosser Street, Park Village. *(Kath Burns Collection)*

David Maybury and John Conway (left), both members of the RAOB today, line up with Bob Stokes and Don Bamford to take part in the Jubilee Civic Sunday Parade on 16 June 2002. David is wearing the sash of the Deputy Grand Primo, Wolverhampton District, while John, formerly of the Royal Tank Regiment, is wearing the sash of the Knights Chapter RAOB. Bob is a former member of the 6th Airborne Division, and Don is chairman of the local Royal Air Force Association. *(Ned Williams)*

The Wednesfield Branch of Toc H first met in 1924 and was granted its lamp four years later, making it the oldest branch in the district. Its companion organisation, the League of Women Helpers, was founded in 1933 and the two groups amalgamated in 1959. The photograph shows the branch performing the Toc H pageant *The Spirit of Light* in October 1950. Les Hughes (far right) plays Scott of the Antarctic. *(Toc H Branch Archive)*

The Wednesfield Toc H members assemble on 1 July 2002. Left to right: Italia Vaughan, founder member of the Women Helpers and now aged ninety-two, Margaret Saunders, Group Secretary (holding the 1928 charter), Joe Sully and Les Hughes holding the banner behind the lamp, and Chris Williams. The banner was made in the 1950s by Edith Weston, who appears in the top picture! *(Ned Williams)*

The first committee of the Bushbury branch of the Townswomen's Guild holds its inaugural meeting in June 1966, having been launched at the local Community Centre on 4 May. Councillor Mrs F. Jones is in the centre, flanked by Mrs Preston, Treasurer (left), and Mrs Stark, Secretary. *(Janice Robson, TG Archive)*

Members of the Bushbury branch of the Townswomen's Guild in May 2002 assemble around the produce table at a branch meeting in the same Community Centre where the branch began life thirty-six years ago. *(Ned Williams)*

Members of the Warstones Section of the Wolverhampton Squadron of Air Cadets are seen here attending their annual camp at Ouston in 1968. In the centre is Flying Officer Barratt, then adjutant of the Wolverhampton Squadron, and on the left in the back row is Flight Sergeant Nicholls, aged seventeen. *(Flight Lieutenant Nicholls Collection)*

Flight Lieutenant Nicholls leads members of the Wolverhampton Squadron of Air Cadets on the Jubilee Civic Sunday parade on 16 June 2002, marching down Wulfruna Street to St Peter's Church. *(Ned Williams)*

The Scout camp at Badger Dingle, organised in 1947 for the 35th Wolverhampton Sea Scouts (Compton). Scout John Golby is joined by Scout Master Jack Atkins and an unidentified relative. *(Gerald Garman Collection)*

Members of the Wolverhampton Sea Scouts join the Jubilee Civic Sunday Parade on 16 June 2002. *(Ned Williams)*

Seven members of the Wolverhampton Grammar School Scout Group were made Queen's Scouts in 1953, out of a total membership of just twenty-eight. They were Ian Bremmer, Martin Riley, Eddie Sergant, Richard Silk, Alan Locke, John Perrin and Fred Shingler. *(Express & Star)*

New uniforms for Scouts and Scout Leaders: Brian Walters, Philip Bryett and Adam Guest show off the new uniforms as they assemble to take part in the Jubilee Civic Sunday Parade on 16 June 2002. *(Ned Williams)*

No. 8 Company of the Wolverhampton Boys Brigade pause to be photographed with their sports cup during their camp at Patshull Park in 1923. *(Angela Russell Collection)*

David Slater (right), Bernard Pritchett (left) and members of two Wolverhampton companies of the Boys Brigade, wearing their present uniforms, line up at the Jubilee Civic Sunday Parade on 16 June 2002. *(Ned Williams)*

Wolverhampton Girl Guides make their way to St Peter's Church for the Civic Service in May 1927. *(P. Eisenhofer)*

Girl Guides in much less formal attire march past the Mayor of Wolverhampton and his civic party in North Street, after the Jubilee Civic Sunday Service in St Peter's Church. *(Ned Williams)*

The Girl Guide Troop of St Mary's Church, Stafford Street, *c.* 1920. Mary Coxshall is in the top row, third from right, and May Coxshall is in the second row, third from right. *(Gerald Garman Archive)*

Present-day Guide Leaders carry the Fordhouses Troop's flag at the Jubilee Civic Sunday Parade on 16 June 2002. *(Ned Williams)*

The Brownies from
St James's Church,
Horseley Fields, in 1933.
Present are Doris Turner,
Minnie Williams and Vera
Evans. *(Sheila Edwards'
Collection)*

Brownies in present-day
uniform assemble in
Wulfruna Street to take
part in the Jubilee Civic
Sunday Parade on 16 June
2002. *(Ned Williams)*

On 22 June 1990 Ann Poole, the first President of the Wolverhampton Lionesses, receives the group's charter from the District Governor of the Lions, Brian Burgess. It had taken about eighteen months to build up the membership to the required number of twenty and it was a proud night at the Park Hall Hotel when the charter was handed over. *(Lynn Hadley)*

The Wolverhampton Lionesses have remained a small but busy group, which still includes one founder member, Sue Hadley. They have raised over £50,000 for charity in the last twelve years. The picture includes Pat Kempson, Secretary, and Nicola Moore, the current President. They are assembling in Wulfruna Street to join the Wolverhampton Jubilee Civic Sunday Parade on 16 June 2002. *(Ned Williams)*

Members of the Wolverhampton Folk Dance Club in 1928 sit down to have their photograph taken in Queen's Arcade – giving us little idea of their style of dancing! *(Frank Sharman Collection)*

On the other hand it is not so difficult to imagine the dancing style adopted by members of the Wolverhampton & District Caledonian Society. Here we see Andy Duncan (left) and David Dewick (right), President and Secretary of the Society, with their wives Evelyn and Helen on the steps of St Peter's Church after the Jubilee Civic Sunday Service held on 16 June 2002. The society was founded in 1938 by Scottish families living in and around Wolverhampton to keep alive their interest in Scottish culture. *(Ned Williams)*

Members of the Gay Edwardians Old Time Dancing Club (it seemed a good name at the time!) are photographed at their Annual Ball at Wolverhampton's Woolpack Restaurant in March 1960. Their regular Saturday night dances were held at the Bradmore Community Centre. *(Gerald Garman Archive)*

To relive the glamour of Old Time days in 2002 you can go along to the Civic Hall on Friday afternoons and join the weekly tea dance. Steve Tovey, the City Organist, is seen here on 7 June 2002 at the console of the mighty Compton organ with three of the tea dance regulars, Hilary Lewis, Margaret Dudfield and Esther Connah. *(Ned Williams)*

Meeting the stars at Wolverhampton's Grand Theatre is always exciting. In February 1964 Avril Noon, the *Wolverhampton Chronicle* Queen that year, had the opportunity to meet Frankie Vaughan. In the same month one could queue up at the stage door of the Gaumont to meet Joe Brown, Cilla Black or Gerry & the Pacemakers. If you could wait until March there was a chance to meet the Rolling Stones. *(Avril Noon Collection)*

Wolverhampton's Grand Theatre is filled every night when the pantomime comes to town. On 2 May 2002 stars of the forthcoming 2002 pantomime come to launch ticket sales at the theatre – and to meet the audience in advance. Kathryn Rooney (Snow White) and Paul Hendy sign autographs for Jay Harris from Lower Gornal. *(Ned Williams)*

Wolverhampton is a very musical town with many bands, orchestras and choirs and a successful Youth Orchestra – and all that can't really be summed up in two quartets! However, here is the quartet that used to accompany silent films at the Olympia Cinema in Thornley Street, which opened in March 1910. Charles Lowe, pianist, E. Cadman on clarinet, William Bowyer on violin and Walter Fisher on double-bass were photographed on 17 September 1916. *(Jane Parker Collection)*

Less than a hundred yards from where the above photograph was taken we find the Cadenza Quartet playing at the Light House Cinema on 17 June 2002. Charlotte Round, Natalie Reynolds, Suzanne Gee and Matilda Chillingsworth are all ex-Wolverhampton Girls' High School pupils. They are playing at an event to launch the 2002 Wolverhampton Arts Festival. *(Ned Williams)*

Football mad! Like many Wulfrunians, Edward Burns has had a lifelong interest in football. He played football in the Army and later when he was employed in the Wolverhampton Council Public Works Department he supported the department's team. In his fifties he became a linesman and remained one for at least a decade, although his support for Wolves and his loyalty to a works team sometimes caused a conflict of interests! In this 1982 picture he appears on the far right. *(Kath Burns Collection)*

On 20 July 1999 Ted celebrated his Golden Wedding anniversary by going to watch Wolves play Liverpool at Molineux. Ted and his wife Kathleen met both Jack Hayward and Steve Bull, with whom he was photographed. *(Express & Star)*

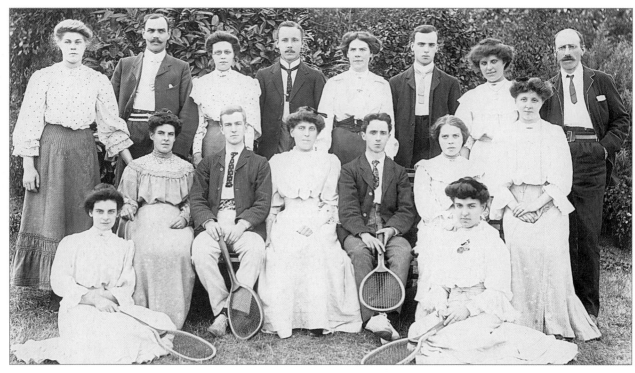

Anyone for tennis? Members of the Fellows family and friends pause to have their photograph taken by Mr Ham, the Wolverhampton photographer based in Mander Street, in about 1908. The family lived in Bilston Street near Monmore Green, and may have played tennis in East Park. *(Audrey Evans Collection)*

Members of the Albert Lawn Tennis Club break off their game to be photographed in the bar of their new pavilion in July 2002. Present are Norman Brookshaw, Bob Fearn (President), Malcolm Ferguson, Lee Guest, Douglas Cooper (Secretary), Jill Dodds (Treasurer), Peggy Ratcliffe and Angela Mann. The ALTC grew out of a club which used courts in Albert Road associated with the Clyno Company, and moved to the present location in Aldersley Road in 1922. *(Ned Williams)*

ALTC members Ollie Wade and David Evans shake hands with their opponents in the 1960s – in the days when one wore white to play tennis. On the skyline can be seen the 'Three Sisters' – the chimneys at Courtauld's factory in Whitmore Reans. (*ALTC Archives*)

Members of the ALTC clear the car-park section of their site in Aldersley Road in the 1980s. Since the war a steady stream of improvements have been made to the club's grounds and facilities. Electricity was laid on, a phone installed, a bar built and the changing rooms improved and cleared of mice. New hard surface courts have been laid and floodlighting installed. Up until 1998 the pavilion was still basically an old army hut but this has now been replaced with the aid of a National Lottery grant. (*ALTC Archives*)

At Wolverhampton's Territorial Army Barracks in Fallings Park an enamel sign is preserved as a piece of local history. The sign invites new recruits to enlist at their 'nearest Post Office' to serve King Edward VIII and it can have been in use for only a short time before the abdication in 1937. The lettering in the bottom right-hand corner of the sign indicates that it was manufactured by the Wolverhampton Chromomatic Sign Company – a local firm operating on Dudley Road. *(Ned Williams)*

Sergeant-Major Hamilton, Sergeant Linva McIntosh, and Staff Sergeant Mick Babb of the 210th Battalion Royal Artillery, based at Fallings Park, pictured outside St Peter's Church at the Jubilee Civic Parade held on 16 June 2002. Sergeant-Major Hamilton had organised the whole parade. *(Ned Williams)*

Coming to Wolverhampton

In the nineteenth and twentieth centuries Wolverhampton became both a popular destination for people seeking work and a good place to live. It still is. This photograph was taken in the Goodyear factory on 10 June 1988 as Salvatore Maragliano from Italy shows off his Medal of Merit for work with the Italian community to Jamha Chadda from India, Pascal Moore from Ireland, and Frank Bodo from Hungary. *(Express & Star)*

James Quirke left Dublin towards the end of 1939 and came to Wolverhampton to enlist. The Labour Exchange told him he would have to work here for a year first so he worked at Jenks & Cattell for twelve months and then joined up. In the meantime he married local girl Kathleen Addison on 2 November 1941 at St Patrick's Church. *(Kathleen Quirke Collection)*

After the war James Quirke never returned to Ireland. He worked at Hill's in Temple Street, where he was photographed in about 1952. His son, also James, has produced a definitive history of Catholicism in Wolverhampton. *(Kathleen Quirke Collection)*

All around Wolverhampton are buildings that reflect the city's cultural and ethnic diversity. The synagogue in Fryer Street was built in 1858 and slightly modified in 1903 after a fire. In recent times the remaining Jewish community in Wolverhampton has not been able to maintain a congregation and the synagogue has now been sold to the St Silas Continuing Church Trust. *(Ned Williams)*

The 'Particular' Ukrainian Church in Merridale Street is much more modern and celebrates the millennium of the Ukrainian Church itself: 988 to 1988. The Ukrainians came to Wolverhampton after the Second World War, at a time when many thousands of people from central Europe were displaced. *(Ned Williams)*

Some Italians also came to Wolverhampton after the Second World War, usually on four-year contracts to work for companies like Brockhouse Foundries or the National Coal Board. St Peter's and St Paul's Church provided a natural meeting place and social focus for the growing Italian community, many of whom had come in groups from the same villages. Here Salvatore Maragliano (*see* p. 99) stands on the church steps with friends in 1956. (*Salvatore Maragliano Collection*)

After church on Sunday, they would stretch their legs in West Park, where these Italian girls posed for the photographer in about 1956. Most of them came to work at the Courtauld's factory in Whitmore Reans, taking up the four-year contracts the firm offered to 'Young healthy girls willing to work'. Some returned to Italy after merely one year, having earned enough for their dowry, but others stayed and stayed . . . (*Maria Maragliano Collection*)

On 15 February 1958 three Italian couples were married at St Peter's and St Paul's Church. From left to right the brides are: Maria (Finatti), Luciana and Armida, all of whom had come from the same northern Italian village, Torviscosa. Only Maria still lives in Wolverhampton, having married Salvatore from southern Italy. *(Maria Maragliano Collection)*

Some of the congregation of the Italian Pentecostal Church in Gorsebrook Road (*see* p. 66) grouped around the Pastor Giuseppi Casa on Sunday 14 July 2002. Giuseppi worked at Goodyears for thirty-two years and retired in 1993. *(Ned Williams)*

The Polish community in Wolverhampton was also established as a result of postwar migrations and resettlement. Its members published histories of their experiences in Wolverhampton after forty years and after fifty years – both books are, of course, in Polish. National costume (with many local variations) and songs have helped them to maintain and celebrate their cultural identity, as seen in this 1960s photograph. *(Jan Glogowski)*

In this 1990s photograph a Polish choir is performing at the Polish Church established on the Stafford Road (*see* pp. 60–1). *(Jan Glogowski)*

Poles celebrate Corpus Christi with a procession at the new Polish Church. The procession includes their own Scout and Guide troops. *(Jan Glogowksi)*

In recent Corpus Christi processions the girls are still to be seen in Polish national costume outside the church in Stafford Road. *(Jan Glogowski)*

Every newcomer to Wolverhampton has a story to tell: Shiro Wattabiki – seen on the extreme left of this picture of the Mizuno Troupe – was a Japanese acrobat born in 1897. He left his family to travel the world with the Mizunos, coming to Britain in 1913. He then travelled to Europe. By the 1920s he had joined Broncho Bill's Circus & Wild West Show, run by John Swallow and based at Gorsebrook Road, Wolverhampton. *(Shiro Wattabiki Collection)*

Shiro Wattabiki met a Wolverhampton girl – Jessie Male – who travelled with the Broncho Bill show as nanny to John Swallow's children. Shiro and Jessie, seen here, were married on 2 December 1922, and had three children. At one time Shiro ran a fish and chip shop in Culwell Street, and later worked at Zinc Alloys in Shakespeare Street. He died in October 1972. *(Shiro Wattabiki Collection)*

In 1960 22-year-old Doris Frith went into a photographic studio in Mandeville, Jamaica, to record her appearance before setting out, with mixed feelings, for a new life in a distant town called Wolverhampton. Although looking forward to a new life with her boyfriend Silbert Griffiths (they married in 1961), she had little idea of the problems that lay ahead in finding housing and work. Eventually Doris found work at Penn Children's Hospital and put in twenty-eight years for the Health Authority. *(Doris Griffiths Collection)*

Doris Griffiths in 2002, running a Day Centre at Lanesfield for Age Concern. Doris is pictured with Jo Newey, a Workers Educational Association tutor who runs classes at the centre. Stan grapples with the Singer sewing machine during a cushion-making session. *(Ned Williams)*

The three Samuels girls on the left were photographed in Jamaica wearing clothes and shoes that their father had sent home from Wolverhampton, where he had gone in search of work. On the right is Sandra, who came to Britain with her sisters in June 1970 to join her parents. Sandra, who was then twelve, remembers being met at the airport by her parents who brought them anoraks – a type of clothing she had never seen, or needed, before! Her sister's reaction was, 'We're not going to like it here.'

Lower left: The Samuels family established in Wolverhampton in 1973. Standing, left to right: Sandra and her sisters Lavern and Marcia; seated: Andrea, Sydney and Alison. Of the six, only two have remained in Wolverhampton. Lavern lives in Canada, the others in London.

Below: Sandra Samuels attended Northicote School and Wulfrun College and expected to have a secretarial career. However, following her mother's suggestion, she decided to take up nursing, and has now spent twenty-six years working locally in the National Health Service. Sandra's life has bound her ever more closely with Wolverhampton. She has sought to serve the community, became a school governor, chaired a local regeneration scheme and has entered local politics. *(Sandra Samuels Collection)*

Sandra Samuels, May 2002, canvassing on an elector's doorstep while seeking election to Wolverhampton City Council in Park Ward. *(Ned Williams)*

The changing role of Wolverhampton in the lives of its inhabitants is well illustrated in the Grant family. Hermine, second from left, came to Wolverhampton in 1961 and remembers wishing that she could return home immediately! Interestingly, her mother did just that and retired to Jamaica. However, Hermine has stayed and established roots in the city. Her daughter Jennifer, sitting next to her, was born in 1968 and grew up in Wolverhampton, attending Grove, All Saints' and Colton Hills Schools. Chris (back row) and Jennifer's children, Lauren and Dominic, complete the picture.
(Ned Williams)

Sukdev Singh Sanghera came to England on 23 March 1966 at the age of fifteen, to join his father. At the time he possessed all of £1.50 but was keen to make his fortune in Wolverhampton. His first job was selling eggs from door to door and then he moved on to selling cloth, working at the markets by day and driving a delivery van by night. In about 1983 he started a dairy business. On the first day he delivered twenty bottles of milk but soon built it up to 14,000 bottles a day. In 1988 he and his brother Jaswant started CS Motors in Cousin Street, and in 1991 bought a bigger garage in Marston Road. Sukdev married Mohinder Samra on 26 March 1972. Above: he leaves his home in Craddock Street; left: Sukdev and Mohinder leave the temple. *(Family Collection)*

Sukdev Sanghera in the 1980s in Craddock Street, with his Express Parcels delivery van, which he drove at night, in the background. *(Family Collection)*

The Sanghera family in 2002 outside their Westland Road home. Left to right: Jasbir Sanghera, Vijay (Jaswant's wife), Mohinder and Sukdev Sanghera, and Jaswant Sanghera. Sukdev would be the first to admit that his progress in Wolverhampton has been very much a family affair to which his brothers Jasbir and Jaswant have contributed greatly. *(Kulraj Sanghera)*

In recent years incomers to Wolverhampton have included people from Kosova and the Middle East. West Park provides opportunities for incomers to encounter the mysteries of living in Wolverhampton with its Vintage Transport Show in June and the City Show in July. From such events they learn that the steam traction engine is still alive and well in Britain and that jousting is still a popular form of entertainment! Mr H. Mirawdali, who came from Iraq nine years ago, has brought his family along to see the sights in West Park. *(Ned Williams)*

Sultan Rabani (centre) from Afghanistan joins some Red Indians in their camp in West Park in June 2002. Steve Horbach (left) and Geoff Payne are champion Indian hoop dancers. Until he came to Wolverhampton, Sultan had never met an Indian hoop dancer! *(Ned Williams)*

For Better & For Worse

On 6 March 1943 Margaret Bowen of 49 Dunstall
Road married Leading Aircraftsman Henry Anthony
Brownrigg of St Johns, Newfoundland, at St Peter's and
St Paul's Church in North Street. At the end of the war,
exactly three years later, Harry returned to
Newfoundland on a US aircraft carrier. Margaret set sail
from Liverpool eleven days later on a ship carrying 400
war brides to America, and another 400 to Canada.
Over half a century later Margaret can still recall her
life in Wolverhampton in detail, particularly her short
career in the Wolverhampton Co-operative Society. As
far as is known, only one other Wulfrunian 'war bride'
went to Newfoundland. *(Margaret Brownrigg Collection)*

On 4 August 1906 Joseph Fellows of 281 Bilston Street married Florence Clara Jackson at St Matthew's Church, Wolverhampton, and this fine photograph was taken by Mr Ham of Mander Street. Next to the bride is her new sister-in-law Gertie, and next to Gertie is the bride's brother Samuel Jackson. The Fellows family ran a nearby ironworks in what was often described as one of the grimiest parts of Wolverhampton. *(Audrey Evans Collection)*

Hubert Hubbard married seventeen-year-old Sarah Jervis on 3 August 1914 and then left for the trenches. Throughout the war he carried with him a picture of Sarah, taken two years earlier when she was fifteen – and the battered and much creased print still survives in the family's archive! *(Moya Lloyd Collection)*

Mary Eleanor Coxshall (last seen as a Girl Guide on p. 88) stands with her mother Hannah in the back garden of the family home at 20 Herbert Street on 21 December 1929. They are about to set off for Mary's wedding at St Mary's Church in Stafford Street (*see* p. 66) where she will marry John C. Garman. No photographs were taken after the ceremony. The wall behind them separated the garden from Russell's Brewery, which was closed even at that time. The house, the church and the brewery have all vanished from the Wolverhampton landscape. *(Gerald Garman Archive)*

On 21 August 1948 Kathleen Reed married Ted Burns (*see* p. 95) at Holy Trinity Church, Heath Town. It was a wedding on rations despite the fact that the war was over. Kathleen's wedding dress had previously been worn by her sister, and the bridesmaids' dresses had to be bought second-hand. They sat down to a wedding meal of cold meat and salad, and the guests had to contribute ration coupons to purchase the ingredients for the home-made wedding cake. The week's honeymoon in Malvern cost 8 guineas. *(Kathleen Burns Collection)*

On 28 October 1961 Anna Vecchio married Giuseppi Casa at the Dunstall Road Baptist Church. The reception was held at the Town Hall Tavern. Giuseppi had come to England to work at Brockhouse Castings, after which he worked at Goodyears for thirty-two years. Anna's story was unusual: her father had been an Italian PoW who returned to Britain after repatriation to be employed on the farm on which he had worked while a prisoner. *(Anna Casa Collection)*

In September 1963 Anna Sacco married Ignazio Divingenzo at the Revival Church in Pipers Row. *(Anna Casa Collection)*

On 1 August 1981 Sandra Marcella married Karl Samuels at Bushbury parish church. There were seven bridesmaids and the groom had six attendants in grey morning suits and toppers. The reception was held at the Connaught Hotel. *(Sandra and Karl Samuels Collection)*

Kalvinder Singh Sanghera's wedding in March 2002 took place over three days. We see him here on the first day at the family home in Westland Road, Wolverhampton. Female members of the family are going through a blessing ceremony in which Kalvinder is rubbed with a yellow dough. On the left is his mother, Mohinder Kaur Sanghera. *(Family Collection)*

On 31 March 2002, the third day of the wedding, Kalvinder and his bride Amardeep are pictured in the foreground festooned with garlands. Behind him are his parents, Mohinder and Sukdev (*see* p. 110), his brothers Gurrajeet and Kulrajdeep and his cousin Harveer. The family never forget Kalvinder's brother Ravinder who died in a car accident in 1996. *(Family Collection)*

Jubilee

The Queen's Arms in Graisley Row, on the Hollies industrial estate, went in for celebrating the Queen's Jubilee in a big way. Licensee Shirley Allen confessed to having mounted celebrations for previous jubilees, and is seen here on 3 June 2002 surrounded by revellers. *(Express & Star)*

The Queen's Golden Jubilee of 2002 prompted many people to recall events of the Silver Jubilee in 1977 and the Coronation year, 1953. Here we see Wednesfield fishmonger Ron O'Brien, trading as H. Kendall, putting on the jubilee style in 1977. He said he spent £500 on his celebrations. *(Express & Star)*

At a party held in Atherton Road to celebrate the Silver Jubilee of 1977 the Mayor of Wolverhampton, Councillor Mrs Jessie Beddoes, found herself having to take on the role of waitress. *(Express & Star)*

Fancy dress competitions seem to be a compulsory part of jubilee parties. Some of the children seen here in Fairview Road, Penn, in June 2002 have dressed up while some are content to wave a Union Jack. The child on the right is red, white and blue toothpaste and brush! *(Express & Star)*

The distinction between may queens, carnival queens and coronation queens seems to have become confused. This young lady was the may queen at Stow Heath Junior School in 1953 – coronation year – but the crown is definitely a reference to the royal crown being worn by the new queen that June. *(Stow Heath Primary School Archives)*

At the Golden Jubilee celebrations of 2002, held at the Old Vine Inn in the Vauxhalls on 4 June, Jeane Hallam's crown definitely follows the same tradition. *(Gudmund Aarseth)*

Back in 1953 street celebrations were widespread. Irene James is seen here as the 'Coronation Queen' leading a procession of children from Laburnam Road, Stowheath Lane, Lilac Road and Hawthorn Road. An actor appearing at the Grand Theatre came along to crown Irene, and festivities were organised in East Park. *(Express & Star)*

Revellers line up for a photograph outside the Old Vine Inn on 4 June 2002. Left to right: Jeane Hallam, piper Victoria Taylor and other guests. *(Gudmund Aarseth)*

The party at the Old Vine on 4 June 2002 was also a reunion for people who had lived in Chester Street, Whitmore Reans, in 1953. Some travelled back from Australia for the occasion, and the total attending came to 125. *(Gudmund Aarseth)*

Geoff Bangham, landlord of the Old Vine Inn, (right), welcomes the Mayor and Mayoress of the City of Wolverhampton, Councillor Robert Hart and Mrs Sylvia Hart, to his jubilee party on 4 June 2002. *(Gudmund Aarseth)*

Acknowledgements & Picture Credits

Over the years a number of people have generously made photographs available to me. Some of these people have passed away, but I know they provided photographs in the hope that would be shared with others via eventual publication. Others have responded at great speed specifically to my request for photographs for this publication.

Pictures have been credited to their source. This is not the same thing as saying that the pictures were actually taken by that person – they are simply prints in that person's collection. In this situation every effort is made to acknowledge fairly the use of each picture and respect people's proprietorial rights, whether the images be family snaps or commercial photographs. Some pictures are copied from postcards, and I thank Ken Rock and Ian Bott for making their postcard collections available to me. I also wish to thank the Editor of the *Express & Star* for allowing me to reproduce pictures that have appeared in that paper.

In the past I have been grateful for Jan Endean's great work with photographic negatives. It is a sign of the times, and changing technology, that recent projects have benefited from similar skills that people now bring to working with computers and scanners. Thanks to Wilf Smith and Suzie who have helped in this respect.

Many people contribute to a book such as this, in a great variety of ways, and I would like to thank the following, arranged in alphabetical order. I apologise to anyone who discovers that I have forgotten to mention them. I am also grateful to all those people who co-operated in the taking of present-day pictures:

Gudmund Aarseth, Don Bamford, Eileen Beards, Revd Edwin Brookes, Margaret Brownrigg, Kathleen Burns, Anna Casa, Kevin Cartwright, Pippa Cole, Joan Cooper, Harold and Iris Dale, David Dewick, Sheila Edwards, Audrey Evans, Bob Fearn, Gerald Garman, Jan Glogowski, Jennifer Grant, Doris Griffiths, Michael Hale, Councillor Robert Hart, Bob Harrison, John and Jean Head, Andree and Eddy Hickey, Terry Hickman, Stan Hill, Keith Hodgkins, Sylvia Horton, Jim Houghton, John Hughes, Judi Hughes, Revd Tony Kinch, Jonathan Lewis, Moya Lloyd, Salvatore and Maria Maragliano, John Masefield, Nicky Moore, Paul Nicholls, Jane Parker, Janet Quirke, Janice Robson, Sandra Samuels, Kulraj Sanghera, Ken Southern, Staffordshire Building Society, Steve Tovey, Barry Tranter, Travel West Midlands, Noreen Turner, Connie Walton, Dave Whyley, Beryl John Wilkes, Kiran Williams, Margaret Woodhall.